Released on August 6, 2025

© Zineb Bizriken, 2025. All rights reserved.

Poetry and Prose

Bitterfly Effect

Zineb Bizriken

To the dreamers stubborn enough to follow their dreams

Tragedy

It's a tragedy to believe in words that don't align,

It's a tragedy to conform and for it to feel right,

It's the death of a soul, of individuality,

A star looses its shine every time it happens,

The sky darkens for the sun takes distance,

It burns of desire for a world that lights itself,

It's a tragedy to repeat the mistake of others,

Knowing they're unhappy yet surviving,

It's all they strive for,

That in itself is a tragedy.

Zi.B

Options

no options in sight
you may say
therefore it is
no options in the field
field of vision

options are countless
from my alchemist eyes
there are even options in the dark
you could say I have night vision
I'm always
semi-sane
semi-insane
were I only one of these
I'd be doomed
blind and ready to forfeit

Zi.B

Here now

You're here now
a dot on the map
here too is a destination
which others attempt to reach
you seek to find someone's here too
isn't that amusing?

Is happiness forever a place to reach
or is it gone unnoticed by the chasers?

Here or there
doesn't really matter
just a question of company
or plainly a state of mind.

You're here now

Zi.B

Trophy Mantra

Everything is my win
it begins and ends as a win
I am a winner
in all that I do
it is my identity
I'm all that I truly need
for the external world
is susceptible to my mind
and reflects what I already see
the trophy.

Zi.B

Twisted

Assumptions are bold twists,
they coil and coil,
till their world turn into cords,
they spiral till it's all in knots,
the world is tied in bold beliefs,
shaped by uncompromising, blind minds,
the cost of blissful ignorance adds up,
they're not willing to pay the bill.

Zi.B

Wildfire skies

Wildfire smoke keeps me indoor
the sky is dull like it was in winter
nature's blues are unlike its colourful nature
I feel like a historian with pictures of the blue sky
on my phone
unknowingly I was treasuring a sight soon to be
scant
faded
muted
hazy
I remember how it was prior
but I don't want to remember
to have to
I want to see it everyday
and be guaranteed tomorrow comes with it
or I'd rather not have tomorrow at all
it'd be an uninvited guest
and I'd be a terrible host.

Zi.B

Faceless introduction

overlook my flesh
for I'm not trying to impress
I do care for myself
don't misunderstand

a glimpse of my mind
and you'll fail to notice the rest
these pages are my eyes
my nose, lips, and ears

my profile written in prose
adorned by crafted metaphors
a tell all that knows me better
an archive of memories
bottled feelings I've let go of

Zi.B

Your music

Your music sounds like things aligning
it seeps with nostalgia
the moment in a movie
where you feel things may be alright
it's abundant in comfort
an embrace reciprocated through minds
you bridged my wandering thoughts
words you sing make me feel seen
unlocked a part of me I hadn't known was there
were we communicating beyond time
or was that just my wishful thinking
the more I exist
the less I believe in coincidences.

Zi.B

Feeling in a bottle

I trap my feeling in a bottle
then I call it a poem
for it is fleeting
and my memory unreliable

boxes are too rigid
too limited
to understand my feelings

bottles can take the pressure
they can release it too
shake it and it can overflow

my feeling is in a bottle
in hopes I can drink it again

Zi.B

Reciprocated

Reciprocated
the word's a lethal drug to me
I long for it
I'm addicted to a substance I've
yet to taste
It's all I need
It's all I'll ever want
I want it all reciprocated
for one isn't separate from its
opposite
It's one of the same
in a simpler word it's
reciprocated.

Zi.B

Surrender to the flow

Surrender to the flow
doubt and trust
are sides of the same coin
co-existing polar opposites
birthed from a same soil
both a feeling like others
surrender to the flow
the flow doesn't betray
it isn't fickle like us.

Zi.B

The bridge

Our words became a bridge
mirrored halves it took
along with resonance
as well as convictions
charged with emotion
hands holding the rope
we step to the core
home is indeed
where the heart lies.

Zi.B

Refraction

Pursed lips and mellow eyes
your smile knocks at my lips
corners lift for guilt is no more
surprised by the smile you expected
your eyes began to glow
refracting light like never before
you see me like no other
beautifully distorted
in tune with your own beauty.

Zi.B

The forest

I run through the forest
aware of the trees passing me by
bare and slim yet happier than I
alive and unable to overthink
then again they wouldn't understand
they're lucky to be alive
unlucky to not feel so
no use in envying them or anyone
I'll just keep running
or perhaps I'll walk
with my idea of life

Zi.B

Calm

I swung too far into the lows
because I was too calm

I'm on the verge of tears
tears I haven't asked for
I need constant reminders of
my reflection
for the fog in my head fears to
dissipate

I've changed so fast
now look where I am
I'd still like to believe
that all is well
that this is part of the process
to embrace both ends
for polarity is none

with a silver lining
I'll climb back to stability

Zi.B

Lone little cloud

Lone little cloud
floating away in the sky
bright blue canvas
ridden with potential
I see you with my human eyes
I drift away from the ground
grey concrete canvas
where all has a cost
we're alike lone little cloud
it's like looking at a mirror
what separates us is perception.

Zi.B

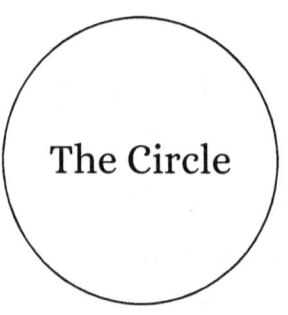

The Circle

You frowned sadly at my words
and I smiled fondly at your frown
those curves joined in a circle
we were never meant to be apart
because circles hold no opening
we live entangled in a cycle
spinning round and round
no end or beginning in sight

Zi.B

Alive Anew

They killed me
I shuttered my dreams
those same dreams
have breathed the life back into
me

lethal words they yielded have
lost power
strings have spiraled into cords
cords no longer connecting
I'm no puppet anymore
and they're no puppeteer

witness the birth of my fantasy
the show's started long ago.

Zi.B

The Void

I fight with the void
create my own problems
voices appear out of thin air
they won't let go
no reasons to fight with myself
I thought.

There's nothing cool about it
this predicament
I'm smarter than this
so why do I keep falling
in the very hole I dug
maybe all I need
is to step beyond the awareness
because I know but I don't do.

Zi.B

Was

No more storms on the way
only continuous stability

I was wrong
I grew so accustomed to that storm
I mistook it for stability
the core of my madness it was

I can't sleep, I keep telling them
but you have to, they tell me

read me a story
put me to sleep
promise you won't leave
not until I've fully drifted

Zi.B

Wounded

The wounded will eventually find me
they'll find me not lonely but solitary
with stitched up wounds and breathing bones
we shall both continue rather than discover
the cycle's energy is transferred but it's the same
same old comfortable cycle which I rely on
the wounded humans found peace
peace that had been resting on their shoulder
waiting for them to notice
to release the burden of ignorance
the real delusion was believing there should be more
when we always had it all.

Zi.B

Pastel cups

Pastel cups stared me down
take us home, they said
that's all you need, they added
I flipped a coin
for I don't trust myself to decide
polar bear meant taking them home
queen meant walking past and never looking back
the coin I'd thrown fell down the drain
I was left standing there
cups still staring me down
I had to settle this myself
voices jumbled together
I couldn't make out their consensus
hesitation added itself to the mix
I had to be the bigger person
If we are meant to be
you'll find me again pastel cups
like the magnets we are

Zi.B

Author's note: On Canadian coins, heads shows the queen's portrait and tails, a polar bear.

Watery eyes

The rain in my heart was so loud
the sky shed those tears for me
my eyes seemed empty
but they held endless oceans
all blocked by a barrage
my sadness was a wolf in sheep's clothing
I mistook it for stability and calm
but I was free falling this whole time
take my hand
bring me back
before my heart drowns in the flood
of my own eyes.

Zi.B

The wolf

The wolf is unclothed
its identity uncovered
doesn't make it any easier
truth be told I'm ill-equipped
I've no armour or weapon
the wolf growls, paws kicking dust
it's no false alarm this time around
war is on the cusp
the wolf cannot be tamed
yet perhaps could be embraced.

Zi.B

The dark

Would it be crazy to enjoy the dark
to find it amusing
enough to chose it over the light
would it be funny to think I'd belong.

The light chased me away
that's a fact
the light was filled with pretense
while the dark was genuine
warmly protective even.

What pulled me was a look
eyes so vulnerable I could cry for them
pain so deep I felt it could cure mine.

Zi.B

Hand

That hand fed you lies
raised you on a sinking mountain
you're going deeper rather than higher
open your mind before you hit earth's core.

Let me be your dealer
find me in the sky
between grey clouds
ascending with rays of sun.

Zi.B

Above the ants

Be above the ants
above the meaning they give
it is not yours
find your own
by that I mean create
similar or not
it doesn't matter
it's unique because it's yours
your meaning is all that matters
be above the ants
you're the only human
in a world of ants.

Zi.B

The butterflies are in effect

Bend the words till they beg for the truth
sort the lies till the score comes running
strip their powers till all is left is regret
slice the loss in half till the wins multiply
ring a bell the butterflies are in effect
their wind howls and echoes in the distance
bitter words sung on a sweet melody
mote it be, they say...

Zi.B

Recycled memories

Tears shed were a drop in the ocean
blaming anyone just plunged me deeper
air isn't scant yet is intentionally taken at times
the desire to surrender is strong but its extent scares me
there are things I'd rather hold on to tightly
memories are a tender subject
each bringing new insight upon reflection
every new version of me has found an unnoticed detail
now again it leaves me in shambles
yet I don't want to let go.

Zi.B

Your younger self

I came across your younger self in a dream
he recognized my sadness and enquired
he didn't mind my reluctancy and gave me time
to unfold my story and the cause of my sadness
his quiet aura which was alike mine brought me ease
in a sea of people that didn't care for my mood
justifiably so
I didn't blame them for I didn't care for theirs either
but I cared about his like he cared about mine
we were closely standing in parallel
in comfortable silence
we'd even watch the wind blow outside the window
we both hated the snow.

Zi.B

About a dead end

A dead-end is an opening
a sign at the end of the road
telling you to go back
for life is a cycle
there is no impasse really
up
down
back and
forth
both ends are part of one road
one road
one way
one shot
a full-stop is never necessary
nor would it be sustainable
all motions are reciprocate
the day starts to end
it ends to start
in chaos
or in calm
but never in a dead-end.

Zi.B

Another day

*Another day in my room
writing at least one more poem
drinking espressos like happy pills
listening to Lana like I've much to hide.*

*Another day wondering if I should step out
perhaps to the coffee shop or the library
the weather's not to my taste
my morale's not up to standards
maybe next week.*

*Another day I can say I'm alive
another one I can look forwards to
another after another
it ends someday
then will be the time to look back
for now
I live*

Zi.B

The page

I kiss the page I am about to fill
fill it with words it didn't ask for
we haven't asked for life either
but we're here, alive, all the same
let me reverse your ashes
page crafted from life itself
trees with roots cemented in soil
let me make sure you're not wasted on us
pardon me for this is the only way
I am able to resuscitate you
I'm aware it's not the same
never will it be
but look at how you live in the minds of so many
look how you live in their hands.

Zi.B

Wolf sheep

The wolf is the sheep
the sheep is the wolf
the disguise is an illusion
I am the wolf
as I am the sheep
boldly vulnerable
quietly loud
a killer who fears to be killed
a victim that once was a
perpetrator
it's never one or the other
I am the Wolf Sheep
and so are you.

Zi.B

Cherry Berry

My cherry
red and plump
choked
and now you're blue
my cherry pie
slipping out
all over
in a curved plate
our cherries
a pair
made to be odd
ripped stem grew back
every time
cherry lovely berry
you're so care free.

Zi.B

Insanity

Write it in reverse
read it properly
describe it colourfully
smear it powerfully
inhale it gently
let it flow in your veins
to the top
trap it there
art is made of insanity

Zi.B

April, 14

April 14, a day to remember
for no particular reason
simply for its existence
one physical hour is left to it
April 14, you'll be longed for
by an overwhelmed version of myself
April 14, 2025
the day you are
the day you were
she'll say
only remembering you through this poem
because perception of time is lost
her hour glass cracked
from how tightly she held it
sand is scattered everywhere
now she relies on the core of her system
the sun
to tell time
April 14, in her mind
you are remembered as greater
just as she desired
you are written over and over again.

Zi.B

My dear anxiety

Pass by, my dear anxiety
there's the way
you're a follower anyways
you don't need a map
just a path
the days where you overshadow logic
are fewer now
the spotlight flickers on you
speak your thoughts
I'll hear all you'll say
they'll be considered
for what it's worth
but know your thoughts don't rule
my dear anxiety
you co-exist with your opposite
the calm
I've been unfair to it
let me consider its thoughts too
let me decide on a case-by-case basis
let me claim my feelings anew
my dear anxiety, you belong
I embrace you like I do the calm
it's alright, my dear anxiety
there's no need to be so scared
the moment will pass
they eventually all do
after you comes relief
only then can I be grateful for you.

Zi.B

Miserably lucky

World of ours
miserable you are
potential you had
fortunate I am
to see your charm
despite the glamour
despite the debris
fortunate I am
to pierce through the lies
to see your root
lucky I am
to love you at last
genuinely this time.

Zi.B

Ghostwriter

I am ghostwriting this poem
for I don't feel like myself
this consciousness is deprived of regulations
I am a conductor with no sense of direction
my custody for this page is temporary...I know
despite the circumstance, I am genuine all the same
if not more
like a drunk crying out

am I waning now?
if so devour me please
you of tomorrow
capture my memory
don't forget me
but don't repeat me

Zi.B

Vaccine

Smoke pours out the streets
it's greyer than foil
you plead, your heart on your sleeve
but the threshold's higher now
traces of the grey are no longer
discreet
they queue in traffic
their privileges revoked
they're a product of you after all
but I'm immune
for I've had enough.

Zi.B

I feel, therefore I am

I live by what I feel
not what I'm told
and in one of
the many endings
they'll tell me what I've
already felt
because that's the cycle
it goes only to come back
and I get to throw the
boomerang
I'm telling you now
I am ready to feel
what I want is what I am.

Zi.B

Liars

Liar liar I couldn't be
It's stronger than I
It isn't part of my identity
I don't criticize you for lying
I'm but amazed at your ease in doing so
how without a blink or the hint of hesitation
you lie
like you believe you're telling the truth
you don't stutter or stumble
as you spit the words out
I'm amazed at myself for not believing you

but now I'm the bad person
as you make is it seem so shamelessly
you made me a liar
my truth is your lie
liars we both are now
the truth is lost
the lie not far behind
what were we even talking about?

Zi.B

Another coffee

Another coffee I've brewed
because the former wasn't bitter enough
"That's better," I mutter from the first sip
the night is off to a better start
but the night wasn't so bad even with weak coffee
"Where is this poem going?" I ask myself
realizing I'm writing about a tiny glass of coffee
I took another sip, hopeful it'll share me a line
alas coffee doesn't communicate with words
and I sit afraid it'll stain my teeth
because you see I mainly drink espressos
the dental hygienist had winced when I told her that
yet understood
she too couldn't renounce coffee
worry not I rinse often with water
and worry not this poem comes to an end
for further lines escape me
and my coffee's getting cold.

Zi.B

My syrup is bitter

Swallowed me like the clouds do the sun
how does it feel to live in my darkness now
does the memory pulse at your feet
when I smiled at you and meant it

is your knowledge recalled or understood?

submerged in my melancholia
tell me do you hear the pleas
are they bitterly coating your flesh
sticking out and hard to wipe
do you still believe you know me?

Zi.B

Bummer

Bummer
is all I can say when it comes to you
what could've been will never be
and that's a bummer
but what can I do
nothing
you might change
but I'm not planning to wait
change for another
or even yourself
I don't care
not anymore
not any longer
It's a bummer, really.

Zi.B

Temporary tattoo

He was a temporary on her wrist
she was well aware he wouldn't last
and as he faded by the day
she stopped waiting by the phone

her mind
polluted by his tendencies
took the time to disinfect
and when came the time to bid farewells
she expected nothing and said everything.

Zi.B

The line

I'm happy for you
and I wait in line
my turn is coming
that's for sure

I hope I'm never out of line
in the way I feel for you
hope I'll never be green with envy
but green with peace

the line seems never-ending
like I'll eternally be at the back
I don't mind it as much
for my resolution to this line
is proof I am alive
the prize is on my side
like it is on the other side.

Zi.B

Crystal Clear

The crystal heart cries
drops hang from the chandelier
the puddle's reflection tells the future
one so predictable it was wasteful
pardon the pun but it was crystal clear
shimmering splendour is lost on us

crystal glass in your hand
ice cubes clinging together
whiskey burning your throat
numbing your sense

wear the crystal mask
hide the tears
charge them with belief

Zi.B

Robbery

It's a robbery
in broad daylight
your time is gone
it'll never come back
for the cycle isn't fair
and you chose to believe so
your belief charged
their power is ever growing
assumptions turned to reality
dreams stray for your magnet is positive
what you call for is what you get
your hands up
you surrender
knees on the ground
to conform
to belong
in the not so well thought of heist.

Zi.B

Rock Playing Vampire

Rock playing vampire drinks blood mercilessly
fangs anchor on skin till ocean-like depts
rock playing vampire fiddles with the bass
strings caused a blood bath
gathered into blood bags
the bats dance in the cellar
wings spread like fans
the beat drops
forms a pool of blood
sun is down moon is bright red
smells like iron feels like ecstasy
the world is changed by the rock playing vampire.

Zi.B

In the studio

In the studio
writing a poem
or whatever comes to mind
worries are forbidden
in the studio
a world away from reality
time stops in the studio
nothing matters here
laws are void
society's a daydream
the news a fantasy
a waste of time
people's opinions
a whisper in the distance
the studio
is an extension of my head
additional space for my racing thoughts.

Zi.B

Save her

The UFO has landed on the avenue
in the middle of the quiet night
when everyone rested unconscious
all except her who couldn't sleep
she stared out the window
like there laid the cure to her insomnia
written in the sky amongst hazy clouds
a tell all constellation maybe
instead she noticed the UFO
its lights flickered until they ceased
and as though bowing to it
street lights followed shortly after
plunged with somberness
all she could see were sparkling beings
they walked out indiscreetly
"take me," she whispered
the sparkling beings faced the moon
"I am nothing to them without merits,
without light," she added
the conspicuous beings reached for the moon
landed amongst streetlights
even they couldn't save her.

Zi.B

Sand castle avalanche

The sand castle collapsed
it was an avalanche
in mid July
the treasure buried underneath
was freed
until a crashing wave dragged it away
now claimed by the ocean
the treasure cursed the sand
longed for wings
wished to be taken by the clouds
the treasure could not fall farther
though they say the lows make the highs higher
and so the treasure was hand picked
by a grey bird who flew too close to the sun
the treasure lost its shadow to the brightest star
a rite of passage
the grey bird called it
exhausted
the treasure called for a middle ground
the poet tells it that part's not figured out yet.

Zi.B

She's cool

She's cool, there's no denying it,
laying on her bed
looking for flickers in the night sky
listening to her dark RnB
dreaming of her reality
forgoing their words
as much as she loves words
she loves them pretty
shallow much?
nonetheless she's cool
sipping on her espresso
scrolling down endless photo albums
the night is younger than her
yet has more wisdom
but is it cooler than her?
no one could be
not the night
not anyone.

Zi.B

Guilt

The world feeds me guilt
let me spit it out
it's not mine to shoulder
I'm the executrix now
I choose your mask
wear it proudly
step down
let me walk on you
it's not revenge
it's what's natural
treat others as you would yourself
let me treat you
to that same meal you cooked me
chew
swallow
digest it if you can
or choke if it's beyond you
I don't care as much as you did.

Zi.B

In, with

I'll be smoke without fire
in chaos
with love
I'll think less and expect more
in serenity
with butterflies
I'm not looking for hope
(that is forever out of reach
for my longing puts distance)
in space
with circulation

writing without purpose
lets the purpose find me
and it has

Zi.B

Bottled Slumber

You're like cigarettes to me
they're cool, but I don't need them
you're like the sun to me
it's warm, but too much of it burns
you're like a hit song to me
played it for days, now I skip it

you're nothing new, ancient to me now
not by age or regular time perception
just old news shelved in the archives

sour candy of my mine, you've sunken
to depths of my mind I dare not reach
buried
not forgotten
yet not thought of
bottled in slumber
are you dreaming of me there?

Zi.B

Uh, oh, my coffee

I spilt my coffee
it's hot to the touch
hard to watch
I'm quick to wipe
it's hot to the tongue
bitter after-taste lingers
all is well eventually
it deserved to be written
doesn't need to rhyme
my coffee's cold now
and I'm not any bolder
just tempted for another.

Zi.B

Chained to my reflection

Convicted not convinced
old ways are the easiest
they were right
life indeed is hard
but they're all walking backwards
what can you see in reverse?
the back of another perhaps...

freedom they speak of
but they form a chain
a chain of self destructive beliefs
don't drag me there
I've no interest in shackles

I look for my reflection
wandering in time
she tells me:
"Walk in place and you'll still get there."

Zi.B

What can I say

What can I say
What can I mutter
Strapped to the page
I yearn to write
Nothing rolls off
It's hollow in there
Like there's space waiting to brim
Acutely, I crave to write
Cravings are impossible to chase off
Like old habits, they stick
A sticky poisonous mess
Jammed in every crevice
One'd be too lazy to be a meticulous cleaner
It gradually spreads marking its territory
Soaring one minute, deprived the other
What can I say
What can I allow myself to express?

Zi.B

Caution, slippery

Disappointing to say the least
bright to say the most
a mystery slipping away in the flood
the sign is lost in translation
glides a wave at a time
peace is in the air
flying between the drops
turmoil on the soil
the door opens in advance

Zi.B

The fall

Remind me of life's bright side
when the fog wins every war
and I find breathing to be draining
remind me now
I'm forcing every breath
how did I fall back so soon
it took me by surprise
the gap was longer than this
what happened to it
is it shortening like a life span
is it foreshadowing a fall I may not come back from?

Zi.B

Quicksand

I'm too calm for my own good
I suppress more than I need
I resist my individuality while I criticize that lack in others
I'm a cool calm collected mess
the definition of do as I say not as I do

wake up, I utter countlessly
something's missing, I respond
but it's right there, I counter
what's there, I ask
no answer except for the fact nothing's static
I'm stuck, I think
I'm sinking in quicksand

"Don't expect to be pulled out
move with the sand
distribute your weight
it's a slow process
find who it is you're dreaming of."

Zi.B

A message for you

The person I want to thank is, of course, you. You who have read my book. My gratitude to you is endless. I am writing this message with you in mind, imagining we were face to face. Words I'd tell you, I'll write them down. Thank you is the obvious one, but I reckon there's more to it. Having read my book, you perhaps have related to certain poems, and or have understood me more—if you had intended to. You've discovered a part of me I'd seldom share directly with people. Writing allows me to be the most honest version of myself. Otherwise, I'm quite the shy and quiet person. But with written words, I bare it all. If you've made it to the end, I'm assuming I didn't scare you off. So thank you for sticking around. I'm a stubborn person; therefore, I will continue to publish books until I die, and no one can make me yield. But aside from the stubbornness, you are a reason too. Your existence and your choices are quiet reasons for my tenacity.

I'm sure somebody needs the words that I write, is what I tell myself often. There'd be no point in sharing my works if not for the intention of finding people that resonate. Your being here is proof enough that you resonate with me. Welcome to this still unnamed club.

Someday I'll maybe form an organization for us, and we'll share our thoughts and creativity together. I can't wait to see how different everyone is and all that you have to share. Keep your eyes peeled for it.

To end this message, I'd like to say that I'm uncertain when I'll release my next poetry collection as I am currently working on novels. It's been a year since I've struggled with novels, drifted from them, and focused on poetry instead. Now I've returned to my flow and am confident in completing new novels. As for the poetry, I wouldn't know where to fit a new release. I will still write poetry and release it somehow. You probably will find on my Instagram @zi.b.writes occasional poems from now. So, I suppose I'll see you there. Goodbye now, and thank you

Playlist

i bet u callin my name - Mac Ayres
Moon Girl - Ha Vay
NAZARETH - Lana Lubany
Limewire - Julia Wolf
Less Than Zero - The Weeknd
Bluebird - Lana Del Rey
Emily - PLAZA
Mr. Adams - Katerina Lomis
Muse - Sofia Issela
Lose it all - Psylosia
Head Over Heals - Jenevieve
Ice - Faouzia
I can't save you (Kira) - Skye Paula & Od
Music box of fate -StarlightDaryl, Ironmouse & WUNDER RiKU
Possession - King Mala
Lover Girl - Laufey
Avalon - DPR IAN

*I've narrowed it down to one song per artist, but I listened to many more songs from these specific artists. This is an overview of what I listened to while working on this book.

Try writing a poem?
It can be therapeutic

www.ingramcontent.com/pod-product-compliance
Lightning Source LLC
Chambersburg PA
CBHW050344010526
44119CB00049B/693